MW01233718

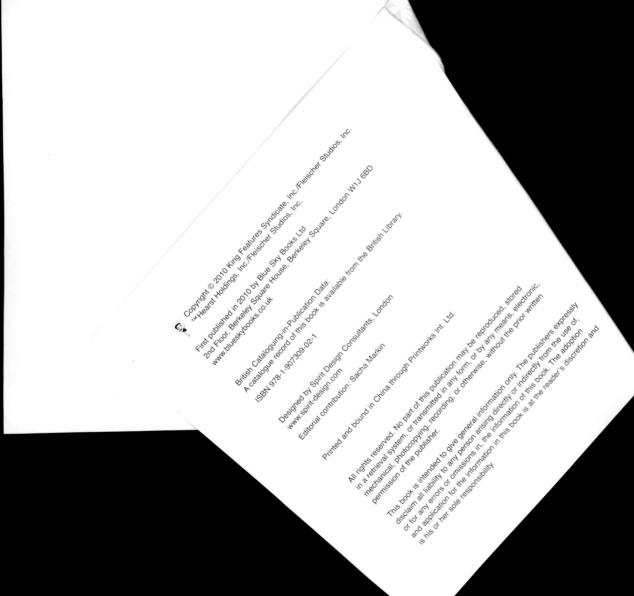

First published in 2010 by Blue Sky Books Ltd
2nd Floor, Berkeley Square House, Berkeley Square, London W1J 6BD
www.blueskybooks.co.uk

British Cataloguing-in-Publication Data:
A catalogue record of this book is available from the British Library.

ISBN 978-1-907309-02-1

Designed by Spirit Design Consultants, London
www.spirit-design.com

Editorial contribution: Sacha Markin

Printed and bound in China through Printworks Int. Ltd.

The secret's out –
Betty Boop
shares all!

blue
sky

Happiness is a new handbag –
heaven!

Giggling until your tummy aches – ouch, stop that!

Wrapping Christmas presents under the tree, nibbling your favourite cookies and drinking something delicious – oh, hi Santa – want to join me?

Having someone tell you you're beautiful – you know you are, but it doesn't hurt!

Painting your nails bright pink – go get 'em girl!

Sipping hot chocolate with squishy marshmallows – yummy, yum, yum.

Making eye
contact with a
cute stranger –
(he's sweet, get
his number).

Silk pillow cases – go away alarm clock!

Kissing your new boyfriend for the very first time D-E-L-I-C-I-O-U-S!

Hot towels fresh from the dryer –
B-L-I-S-S

Warming your tootsies in front of
a log fire – are they toasted yet?

Finding your favourite shoes on
sale (no, you can't buy two pairs!)

Daydreaming... golden beaches, blue lagoons, tanned surfers – oh, pardon me, can I get past, I think this is my stop!

Finding the perfect red lipstick – kiss me quick... or slow!

Falling in love – boop-oop-a-doop!

Enjoying the little things – come here little ladybird, let me count those spots.

A lovely hot shower. Now, where's that soap?

Snuggling in bed with fresh sheets, your favourite pink pyjamas, watching a great movie. PLEASE, DO NOT DISTURB!

Chatting with your best friends. Now, where were we?

Holding hands with someone you love – don't let go!

Treating yourself
to flowers, one
bunch or two?

A picnic for two.

Shining your shoes. Is that me I can see?

Being with happy people – it's contagious!

Sunbathing, eating your favourite ice-cream. Oh, that life-guard's a cutie.

Leaving the salon with a great new hair-style. Where to now?

Dressing up for lunch.

A phone call from the one you love – yes, I'm sitting comfortably.

Your favourite song playing on the radio. I must learn those words.

A sunday lie-in – B-L-I-S-S.

 A weekend getaway with your sweetie – what about a trip to Cloud Nine?

A smile from a stranger – why, I think I might be blushing.

A great big slice of scrummy chocolate cake – yummy, yum, yum, oh another slice!

Dabbing your favourite scent behind your ears. Lovely.

Going somewhere you've never been before. A day trip to somewhere please, I'm so excited.

A stroll in the moonlight – the stars are nearly as pretty as you are.

Treating yourself for no reason.

Laughing and flirting with your boyfriend. Boop-oop-a-doop!

Someone saying thanking you when you open the door. You're most welcome!

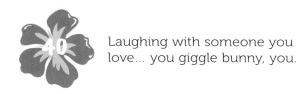 Laughing with someone you love... you giggle bunny, you.

 Happiness is a good hair day. Complete Happiness is a G-R-E-A-T hair day.

Sending a love letter... 'Roses are red, violets are blue, boop-oop-a-doop, means I love you – I do hope he can read!'

Having fun on a shoestring. Remember – any place is nice to be, if you have good company!

HOLD ALL CALLS! Doing nothing on a rainy day but curling up and snoozing... zzzzz!

 Always looking on the bright side – every cloud has a silver lining, oh I just saw it, and it's all shiny.

Shopping 'til you drop... with some pennies left over.

Soaking head to toe in a big, warm bath of frothy bubbles – oh there you are tootsies – one, two, three, four... oh I've lost count, better start again.

Saying thank you when someone opens the door – Miss Manners will be o' so pleased.

Doing work you love. Hold that career ladder, I'm climbing up. Hold it, I said!

Everything falling into place – did I plan that?

Tiptoeing barefoot on soft green grass – wiggle, wiggle, wiggle!

Having someone play with your hair.

Baking a great big chocolate cake
– no, you can't lick the spoon!

A handsome stranger saying hello – is my hair straight, is my lipstick even... oh, where did he go?

 Picking your own bunch of flowers – red and yellow and pink and green, orange...

A party with all your friends... just because you feel like it!

Walking in the sunshine.

Looking beach-tastic!

Going ice-skating, falling down, giggling and getting back up again.

 Enjoying each and every single day – is it bed-time already?

A movie bonanza at home. Relax and enjoy the show. (Sssshhh... it's starting, oh is that popcorn?)

Getting your teeth cleaned. They're so bright!

Finding the cutest heels... that don't pinch at all. H-E-A-V-E-N-L-Y

64

Gazing at the stars – oh look, a shooting one – quick, make a wish!

Finding a boyfriend who's not only good looking, but smart too. Ummm, let me tick all those boxes.

Happy memories... that make you smile!

Giggling for no reason, now I just can't stop.

Taking the perfect picture of all your friends. Smile, sweeties. It's a wrap.

A pillow fight – it's so-o-o-o much fun. What's the score?

 Strawberries and cream – boop-a-licious.

Kissing in the snow.

Learning something new... what's that peeking out of your handbag? Why, I think it might just be a hidden talent.

Doing what makes you happy – yes, sweetie, it's true.

Someone singing you a song... in tune or not...

Wrapping a gift for someone special with pretty paper and bows and ribbon and... lots of love. Boop-oop-a-doop!

Speed walking on heels without spilling a drop of latte.

Eating home grown strawberries. They look much too good to eat.

Finding the perfect
LBD (little black
dress)... nothing
more to say.

Being P-A-M-P-E-R-E-D... any time, any place, anywhere!

Wearing what makes you feel happy.

A school friend remembering your birthday - oh, is that present for me, that's sweet.

A candlelit dinner for two... who said romance is dead? He looks alive to me!

Kissing in the back row of the movies... any night of the week!

Dancing under the stars.

Riding in an open-top with the wind in your hair. Oh yes please, let's go faster!

Shopping! Shopping! Shopping!

A stranger giving up his seat – sit down quick, he may change his mind.

 Dating the perfect gent – wow, he opened the car door, that's so sweet!

Getting a compliment any time – why, thank you so-o-o-o much!

Breakfast in bed – the perfect start to the day. I think I could get used to this!

Happiness is getting a gift you love, from someone you love. Can I open it now?

92

Mixing yourself
a big, creamy,
frothy chocolate
milk shake...
or strawberry...
or vanilla... or...
you choose –
d-e-l-i-c-i-o-u-s

No lines at the supermarket.

Looking great when you bump into your ex – sorry, can't stop, places to go, people to see!

Wearing matching underwear.
I wouldn't expect anything less.

Making a duvet hideaway –
they're gonna have to send in a
search party.

Speaking up, even when your knees are wobbling!

Spending time with your best friends.

Happiness is Boop-oop-a-dooping!

Love,
Betty x

Look out for more secrets from **Betty Boop...**

Dating
Miss Boop's tips on looking date-great! Where should you meet on a first date? Is he Prince Charming or just another frog? Betty Boop is the expert – she's here to help you get it right!

Beauty
How do you get super-luscious lashes? Boop-a-licious lips? The tan-fantastic? Read on and you'll find out.

New You
We all need a boost from time to time. Miss Boop shows us lots of little things that make a very big difference. Juicy fruit drinks, sunny thoughts and healthy tips for a New You, you'll love!

www.bettyboop.com